A TREE ON YOUR STREET

PICTURES BY **BETTY FRASER**

by SEYMOUR SIMON

Holiday House
New York

A TREE ON YOUR STREET

For Eunice

Printed in the United States of America
Library of Congress Catalog card number: 72-92584
ISBN 0-8234-0215-0

HOW TO USE THIS BOOK

A Tree on Your Street was written with the idea of helping you to find out about your surroundings. Perhaps the book will show you some new ways of looking at things and thinking about them. Even familiar objects on your street can become new and exciting when you learn how to explore them in different ways.

Scientists need to know more than just facts. They need to know how to go about getting the facts. That's what this book is really about—the methods that scientists use and that you can use too.

By reading the book and following its suggestions you will learn to observe and measure carefully. You will group similar things together in a way that makes thinking about them easier. You'll begin to use numbers and also ideas about size and shape. You'll see how things change with the passage of time. You'll think about what you see and make predictions about what will happen. In short, you'll work in a scientific way.

New discoveries in science come along every day. But the basic skills, the processes of science, continue in the same ways as before. We hope these skills will open new worlds for you to explore wherever you go, even on your own street.

There's a tree on your street
or maybe just around the corner.
Even a big city has many trees
growing along its streets,
in vacant lots,
or in school yards.

Have you ever looked closely at a tree?
It's full of all sorts of interesting things.
You have to look carefully to find some of them.
A tree changes as the seasons go by.
Each day brings something new to wonder about.

Choose a tree on your street as your special tree. Visit it often so that you can watch how it changes. Look at it in the cool early light of morning, and in the bright heat of the noonday sun. Visit it in the rain and in the snow. Come too at night, to see if any animal visitors make the tree their evening home.

Perhaps you can draw or photograph
the tree or some part of it.
Label each picture with the date it was made.
Compare the picture with the tree at a later date.
Do you see any changes?

Can you reach up to the
lower branches of your tree?
Can you reach to the top branches?
Could your tallest friend
reach to the top?

Can you tell the height of your tree?
Could you use a ruler to measure
the height of your tree,
or is it too tall?
Here's one way you can make a good guess
about the height of a tall tree.
Compare the tree with a nearby house.
A two-story house is about twenty feet high.
An apartment house is about ten feet
from one story to the next.
Suppose your tree reached to the
third story of a nearby apartment house.
How tall would it be?

Do you know the name of the group of trees
to which your special tree belongs?
Look at your tree carefully.
What is the color of the bark?
Touch the bark with your fingers.
Does it feel rough or smooth?

Here's how you can keep a record
of how the bark feels.
You will need plastic clay, plaster of Paris,
water, an empty shoe box, a mixing bowl,
and some old newspapers.
Press a piece of clay firmly
against the bark of the tree.
Remove the clay carefully and place it
face up in the bottom of the shoe box.
At home, spread newspapers over your
kitchen table to keep things clean.
In a bowl, mix two cups
of plaster of Paris with
enough water to make
a thick, creamy mixture.
Pour the mixture over
the clay in the box.
Put the box aside for several hours
until the plaster hardens.

Hint: Clean up any mess you make.

When the plaster is hard,
strip away the box and the clay.
You will have a plaster cast of the bark of your tree.
Take the cast along with you
to another tree on your street.
Compare the bark of the tree with the cast.
Do different kinds of trees
have different barks?

In what season and what month
do the leaves come out on your tree?
Do the leaves change in size or color?
You can keep a record of how a leaf looks
by making a leaf rubbing.
Choose a leaf from your tree.
At home, place the leaf on a table
spread with newspapers.
Place a piece of tracing paper over the leaf.
Using the flat side of a soft lead pencil,
rub it back and forth over the paper.
To make a good rubbing,
tape the stem of the leaf to the newspaper.
Use a light stroke.
Keep one finger lightly pressed on the leaf
to keep it from moving around.
Afterwards, use a soft eraser to remove
any pencil marks outside the leaf's outline.
You may like to make a collection of
leaf rubbings from many different trees.

At certain times during the year
your tree may have flowers and fruit or seeds.

Honey Locust flowers and leaves

Ginkgo flowers and seeds

Norway Maple flowers

American Elm flowers and leaf

Collect any pods that you find
beneath the trees.
Try to match the seed pod with a
leaf or a rubbing from the same tree.

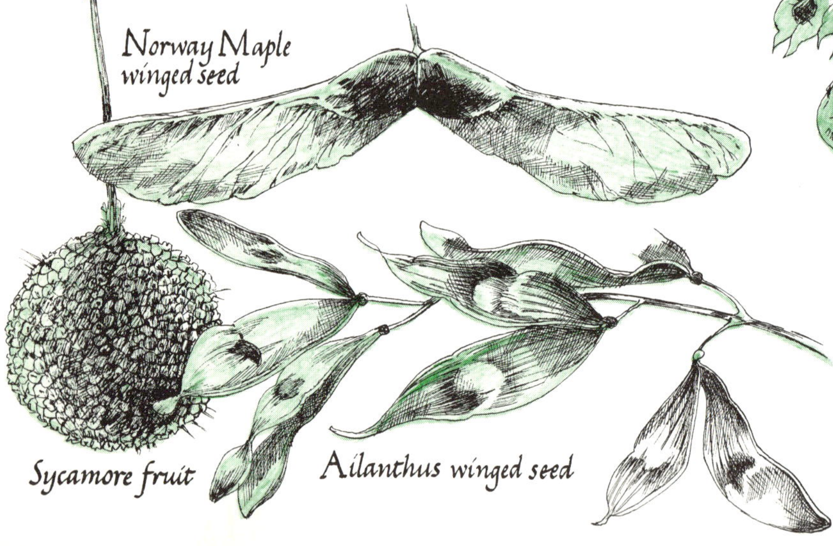

Norway Maple winged seed

Sycamore fruit

Ailanthus winged seed

Pin Oak acorn

The leaf and the seed pod
will help you tell what
kind of tree it is.
Look also at the branches
and the shape of the tree.

Here are some trees that you may find
growing along your street.
You can tell a Norway Maple by the
shape of its leaf and
its winged seeds.

You can tell a
Sycamore tree by
its patchwork bark and
its seed ball.

You can tell an American Elm by its fountain-like shape
and its long slender leaves.

You can tell a Ginkgo
by its fan-shaped leaves
and by the yellow cherry-like
seeds some Ginkgoes bear.

You can tell
a Pin Oak
by its downward
slanting branches
and its acorns.

You can tell a Honey Locust
by its thorns and
its long, twisting seed pod.

You can tell a Honey Locust
by its thorns and
its long, twisting seed pod.

dark streets grow better
t gets the most sun.
ape changes.
erent from other trees
nd that grow in open spots.
such trees?
get enough water during
mer?
and droop
d water.
leaf means your tree
water it needs.
il under your tree.
oil doesn't let water
the tree's roots.
your tree get the
by loosening
r two of soil.
n too deep because
ure the roots.
ı keep the soil loose
summer.

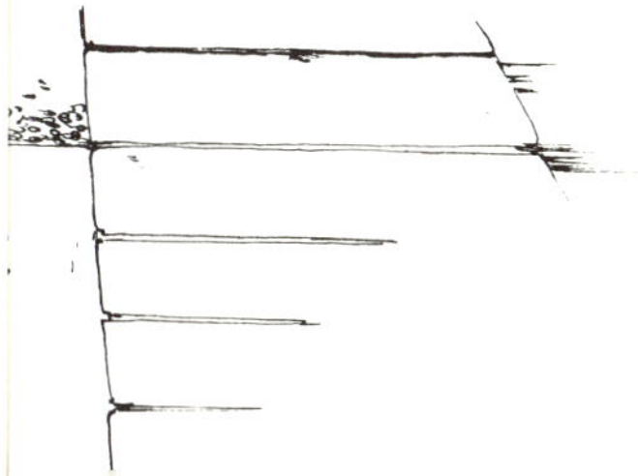

During a very dry summer,
you might want to water your tree.
A young tree needs three or four pails
of water twice a week.

You can tell a Honey Locust
by its thorns and
its long, twisting seed pod.

Some trees on dark streets grow better
on the side that gets the most sun.
Then their shape changes.
They look different from other trees
of the same kind that grow in open spots.
Have you seen such trees?
Does your tree get enough water during
a hot, dry summer?
Leaves curl up and droop
when they need water.
A green, firm leaf means your tree
is getting the water it needs.
Look at the soil under your tree.
Hard-packed soil doesn't let water
seep down to the tree's roots.
You can help your tree get the
water it needs by loosening
the top inch or two of soil.
Don't dig down too deep because
you might injure the roots.
It's best if you keep the soil loose
all spring and summer.

During a very dry summer,
you might want to water your tree.
A young tree needs three or four pails
of water twice a week.

An older tree needs six or more
pails of water twice a week.
Perhaps your friends will help
you carry the pails.
You can tell that your tree has
enough water when a puddle stays
on the surface of the soil
for a few minutes.
Adding more water on top of the
puddle might hurt the tree
by flooding the roots.
It's not a good idea to use a hose
to water a tree. The strong flow
of water from a hose might
wash away the soil and expose the roots.
Try filling the pail with a clean,
quart milk container.
How many quarts of water fill up
the pail? How many quarts of water
does your tree need in a week?

Look for animals or signs
of animals in your tree.
Do birds perch on the branches?
Do they seem to be looking for food to eat?
Watch a bird carefully to see whether
it eats insects or parts of the tree
such as the seeds.

Are there any nests in your tree?
Squirrels as well as birds build nests in trees.
A squirrel's nest is built of leaves and twigs
high up in the branches.

How does the high nest help protect the squirrel?
What kinds of food do you see squirrels eat?
Do you think city squirrels eat the
same foods as country squirrels?

Look for all kinds of insects
creeping and crawling
on leaves and branches.

Also look for insects in cracks in the bark.
Would you expect to find insects
during the winter as well as the summer?

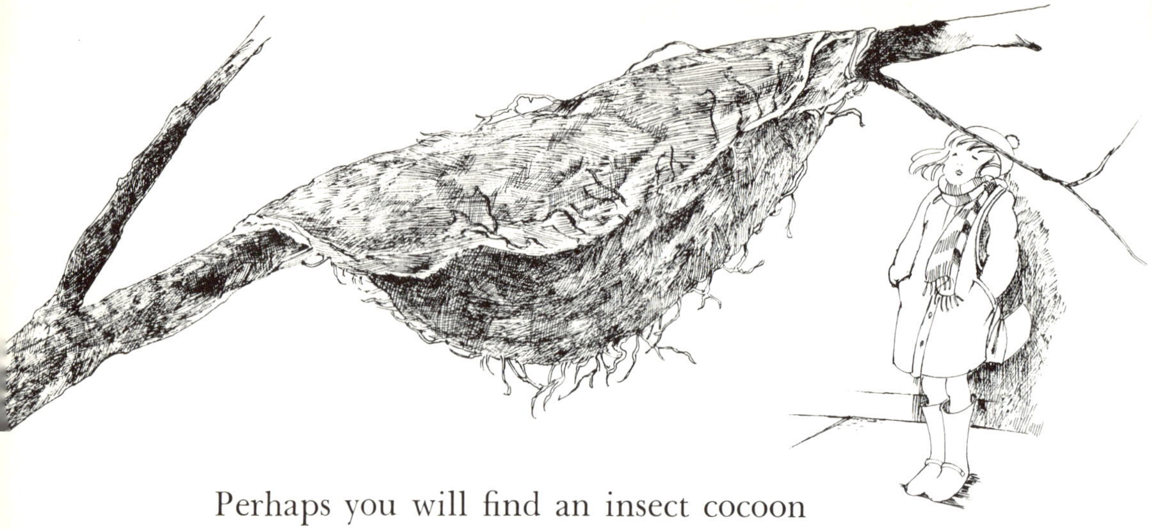

Perhaps you will find an insect cocoon
hanging from a branch during the winter.
What other small animals do you find
in and around your tree?

You might not see the animal but something
it leaves behind,
such as a spider web on a branch
or an earthworm cast on the soil.
A tree means food and shelter for many
small animals.
Can you think of some ways in which
your tree helps any of the animals you spotted?

Sometimes a tree is helped by its animal visitors.
How does an insect-eating bird help a tree?
Can you think of any other animals
that may help a tree?

Sometimes a tree is harmed by its animal visitors, such as caterpillars, gypsy moths, and bagworms.

Dogs and cats can injure a tree
by scratching at the bark.
If there is a badly damaged
tree on your street,
show it to an adult.
Perhaps he will want to call
the Park Department
and ask them for help.

A city tree often shows signs of man and his machines. Sometimes cars scrape the bark of a tree. A truck may break off a low-hanging branch.

Some city trees have a metal fence around their trunks to protect them. Others are protected by a burlap wrapping. Both city and country trees are often injured by rainstorms, heavy snowfalls, and high winds. Sometimes a tree is coated with a glittering shield of ice. But often the ice weighs down the branches until they snap off with a loud crack.

Bark is a tree's protective covering.
An opening in the bark allows insects and diseases to attack the inner wood.
Does your tree have any exposed inner wood?
Poke the exposed wood with your finger.
Soft wood means that it is rotting.

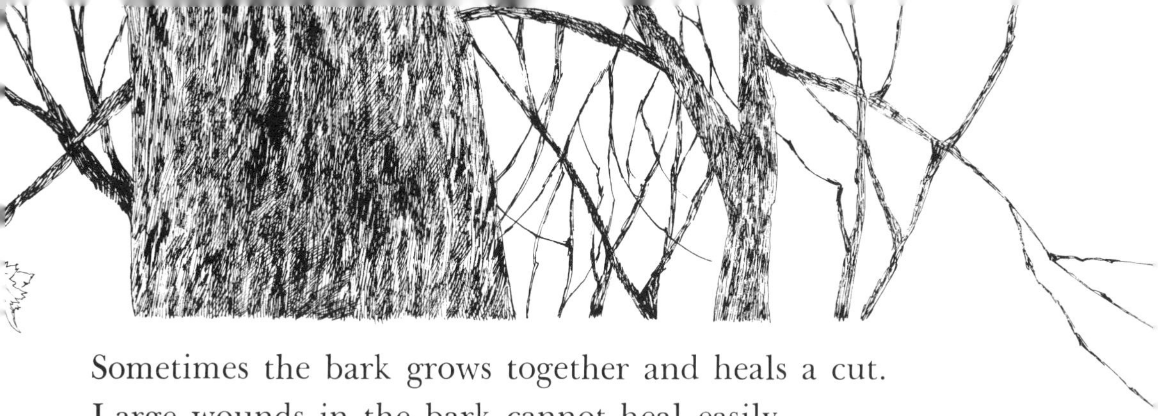

Sometimes the bark grows together and heals a cut.
Large wounds in the bark cannot heal easily.
But if the wounds are treated in time, the tree can be saved.
The rotted wood must be scraped out
and the wound covered with special tar.
Look for wounds on trees that have been treated in this way.
Can you see how the bark starts to grow together?

Sometimes you may see a tall crane
hoist a worker high up among the branches of a tree.
Watch how the dead branches and twigs
are pruned away.
When a tree dies, a new tree
can be planted in its place.
Perhaps you and your friends and neighbors
can get together to plant a new tree on your street.
Write a letter to the Department of Parks or
to the mayor of your city.
Ask about the rules
for planting
a tree on your street.

Each tree is a special tree,
different from all others
yet the same in many ways.
Choose a tree on your street
to be *your* special tree.